Spotlight on the WORLD CUP

Chris Oxlade

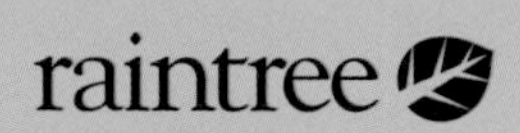
raintree
a Capstone company — publishers for children

Raintree is an imprint of Capstone Global Library Limited, a company incorporated in England and Wales having its registered office at 264 Banbury Road, Oxford, OX2 7DY – Registered company number: 6695582

www.raintree.co.uk
myorders@raintree.co.uk

First published in hardback in 2018
Paperback edition first published in 2018

Edited by Clare Lewis
Designed by Cynthia Della-Rovere
Picture research by Svetlana Zhurkin
Production by Laura Manthe
Originated by Capstone Global Library Limited
Printed and bound in China

ISBN 978 1 4747 5497 2 (hardback)
22 21 20 19 18
10 9 8 7 6 5 4 3 2 1

ISBN 978 1 4747 5499 6 (paperback)
22 21 20 19 18
10 9 8 7 6 5 4 3 2 1

British Library Cataloguing in Publication Data
A full catalogue record for this book is available from the British Library.

Acknowledgements
We would like to thank the following for permission to reproduce photographs:
Alamy: Erik Tham, 22; Dreamstime: Alexey Novikov, 27; Getty Images: AFP/Fabrice Coffrini, 29, AFP/Staff, 21, Bob Thomas, 13, Joe Raedle, 17, Laurence Griffiths, 14, PA Images/Anthony Devlin, 16, Popperfoto, 8; Newscom: Abaca/ Henri Szwarc, 20, AFLO/ Yusuke Nakanishi, 28, dpa/picture alliance, 11 (left), Kyodo, 18, 19, 23, Mirrorpix, 9, 12, Xinhua News Agency/Chen Jianli, 7, Zuma Press/Carl Recine, 24, Zuma Press/Keystone Pictures USA, 10, Zuma Press/Valery Matytsin, 15; Shutterstock: A.Ricardo, 4, AGIF, 25, Anton_Ivanov, 5, Daboost (ball), cover, back cover and throughout, Eugene Onischenko, cover (bottom), fifg, 26, Keattikorn (grass), cover and throughout, photofriday, 6, urbanbuzz, 11 (right)

Contents

Welcome to the World Cup! 4
About the World Cup tournament 6
The history of the World Cup 8
Great players and great teams 10
Great games and great goals 12
Preparing for the tournament 14
The fans arrive 16
The tournament begins 18
Penalty shootouts 20
Fair play and awards 22
The World Cup Final 24
Russia 2018 26
The Women's World Cup 28
World Cup facts 30
Glossary 31
Find out more 32
Index 32

Some words are shown in bold, **like this**. You can find out what they mean by looking in the glossary.

Welcome to the World Cup!

The World Cup is one of the world's greatest sporting events. It is a football tournament for national teams from countries from around the world. The Fédération Internationale de Football Association (**FIFA**) organizes the World Cup.

Germany won the World Cup in 2014, when it was played in Brazil.

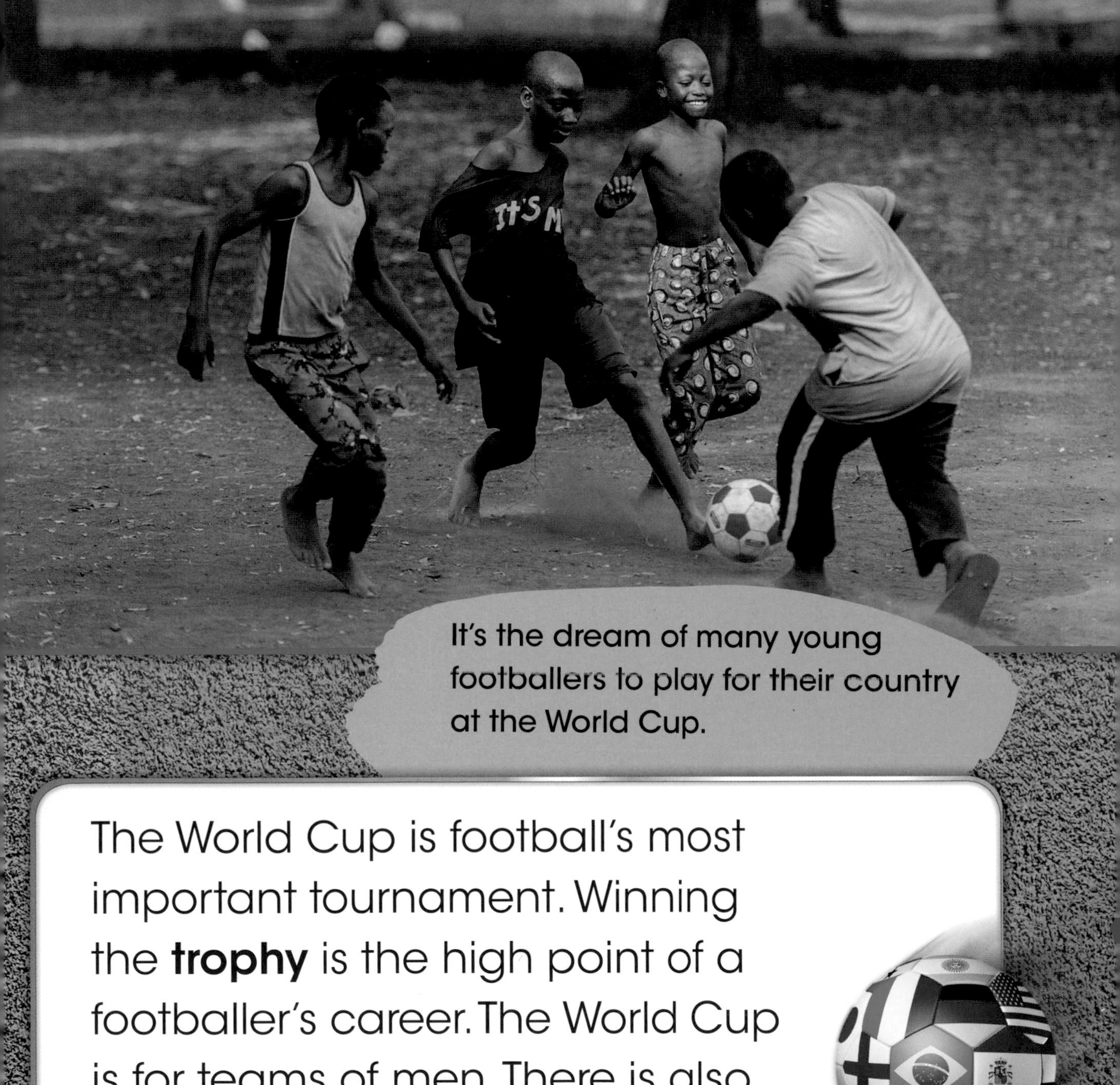

It's the dream of many young footballers to play for their country at the World Cup.

The World Cup is football's most important tournament. Winning the **trophy** is the high point of a footballer's career. The World Cup is for teams of men. There is also a Women's World Cup for national women's teams.

About the World Cup tournament

Thailand and Japan were two of the countries competing for a place in the World Cup in 2018.

The World Cup happens once every four years. Competitions are held in each continent to decide which teams will compete in the World Cup. More than 200 national teams enter. There are 32 places to be won.

The World Cup tournament is held in a different country each time. That country is called the **host country**. Russia is the host country for the next World Cup in 2018.

Brazil was the host country in 2014. Fuleco the Armadillo was the World Cup mascot that year.

The history of the World Cup

The first World Cup was held in 1930 in Uruguay, South America. Only 13 teams played. Uruguay won the tournament, beating Argentina 4–2 in the final. Since then, it has been played every four years except for in 1942 and 1946. This was because of World War II.

Uruguay were the first World Cup champions, in 1930.

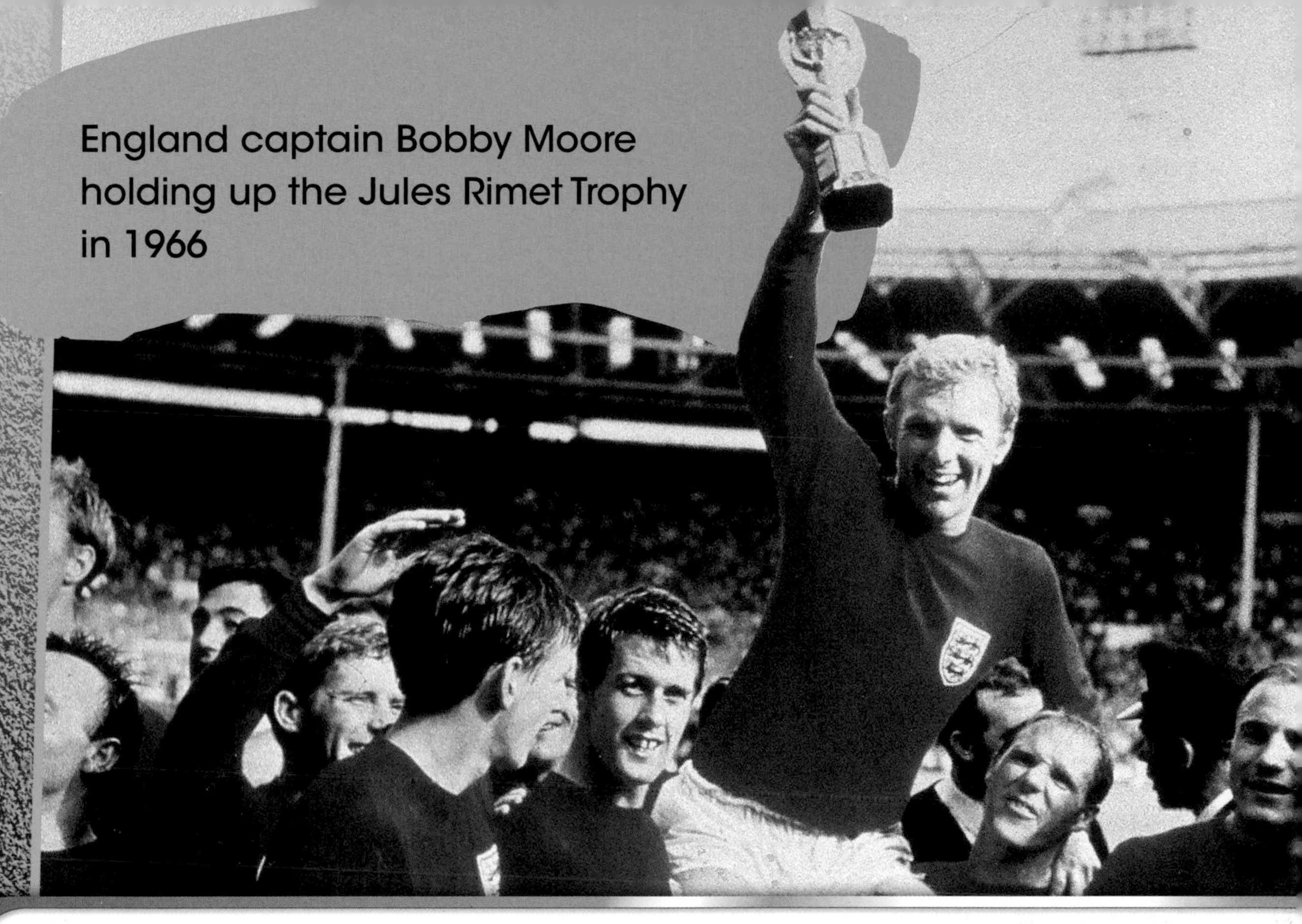

England captain Bobby Moore holding up the Jules Rimet Trophy in 1966

A Frenchman called Jules Rimet first had the idea for the World Cup. The **trophy** was called the Jules Rimet Trophy in his honour. Brazil won the trophy in 1958 and 1962. When they won it a third time, in 1970, they were allowed to keep it. Since then, a new trophy called the **FIFA** World Cup Trophy has been used.

Great players and great teams

The World Cup is a stage for great players to show off their skills. Many players become world famous because of their World Cup performances. They include Geoff Hurst of England. He is the only player to have scored a **hat-trick** in the World Cup Final.

Geoff Hurst scored four goals in total when England won the World Cup in 1966.

Famous footballer Pelé scored many great goals for Brazil.

Many great teams have played in the World Cup tournament. In 1970, Brazil won 12 out of 14 games, and lost only once. In total, they have won the World Cup five times. Germany and Italy have both won it four times.

Great games and great goals

Football **fans** have enjoyed many exciting games of football at the World Cup. One of the best was played in the 1970 tournament in Mexico. Italy beat West Germany 4–3. Five of the goals came in **extra time**!

Fans cheered as Italy beat West Germany in a dramatic game.

In 1974, the Netherlands showed great technical ability. They lost to West Germany in the final but their football made the game exciting for their fans. Every World Cup sees some wonderful goals. There have been unstoppable long-range shots, skilful **free kicks** and amazing **dribbles**.

At the 1986 World Cup, the Argentine player Diego Maradona dribbled past the whole England team to score!

Preparing for the tournament

The **host country** for the World Cup is chosen some years in advance. Normally a few countries apply to be the host. They are called the bidding countries. **FIFA** chooses which of them will be the host.

The FIFA president at the time revealed that Russia was chosen to host the 2018 World Cup.

The host country needs to do a lot of work before the tournament begins. It might need to design new stadiums. It might also need to build new roads and railways so that **fans** can travel to games.

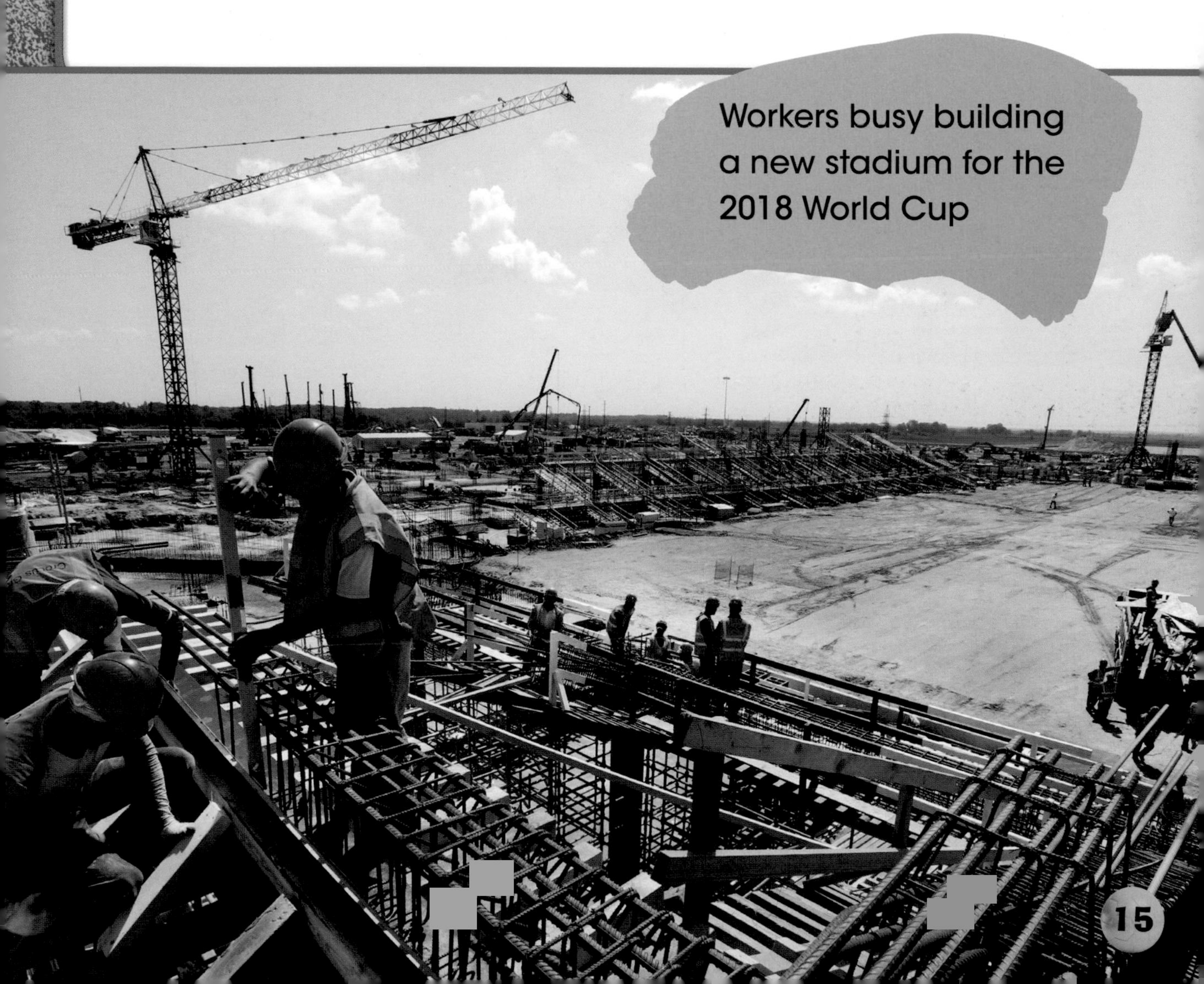

Workers busy building a new stadium for the 2018 World Cup

The fans arrive

Many fans travel for hundreds of kilometres to see their team play.

It's time for the tournament! Hundreds of thousands of **fans** arrive in the **host country** by train, car and plane. They travel to the cities where the teams they support are going to play their matches.

The fans dress up in their team colours. They make a colourful sight in the stadiums. There are special fan **zones** in host cities where the fans can meet up.

Fans who can't make it to the stadiums can watch on television, on the internet or listen to the radio. Families and friends gather together to watch their team's games.

Fans without tickets watch games on giant screens.

The tournament begins

The World Cup tournament starts with a dramatic opening ceremony. The ceremony often shows off the national traditions of the **host country**. There is singing, dancing and people in national costumes.

The opening ceremony in Brazil in 2014 was very lively and colourful.

The tournament teams are divided into groups, which are like mini leagues. The top teams in the groups go through to the knockout stages. The host country always plays in the first game of the tournament.

The opening game of the 2010 World Cup was played between Mexico and hosts South Africa.

Penalty shootouts

Penalty shootouts are very dramatic. If the score is tied after **extra time**, then a penalty shootout decides the winner. Each team has five turns to shoot for the goal. If there is still a tie after that, then it goes to 'sudden death'. Teams take turns trying to score until the tie is broken. It is a very tense way to end a game!

Argentine players watch the penalty shootout in the 2014 semi-final.

West German players celebrate their win against France in 1982.

In 1982, the World Cup had its first ever penalty shootout in the semi-final between France and West Germany. France seemed to be easily winning 3–1. But at full time the game tied 3–3. An exciting penalty shootout followed. Finally, West Germany won.

Fair play and awards

The players, teams and officials at the World Cup have to stick to the rules. They should respect people from other teams. They should set a good example to the **fans**. The team that plays most fairly is awarded the Fair Play **Trophy**.

The Colombian team won the Fair Play Trophy at the 2014 World Cup.

Lionel Messi (right) of Argentina won the Golden Ball award at the 2014 World Cup in Brazil.

There are awards for great performances at the World Cup tournament. The most outstanding player wins the Golden Ball award, and the top scorer wins the Golden Boot award. The most outstanding goalkeeper wins the Golden Glove award.

The World Cup Final

If a team keeps winning its World Cup games, it reaches the quarter finals, the semi-finals and eventually the final itself. The World Cup Final is the most important game in all of football!

Germany and Argentina prepare to play in the 2014 final.

German players celebrate their 1–0 win in the 2014 final.

The team that wins the World Cup Final is the world champion team! It wins the beautiful World Cup **Trophy**, and keeps it until the next World Cup tournament. Celebrations are often held in the winning country. The players are welcomed home as heroes.

Russia 2018

In 2010, **FIFA** chose Russia to host the World Cup in 2018. The tournament will be played in June and July. **Fans** will travel to many different Russian cities to support their teams.

This is the logo for the 2018 World Cup.

The Luzhniki Stadium
in Moscow, Russia

The opening ceremony and the World Cup final will take place at the Luzhniki Stadium in Moscow. About 81,000 fans will be there. The next World Cup will be hosted by Qatar, in the Middle East, in 2022.

The Women's World Cup

The Women's World Cup is for women's national teams. The first Women's World Cup was played in 1991 in China. The tournament has been held every four years since then. Nearly 200 teams try to qualify for a place in the tournament.

The USA won the Women's World Cup in Canada in 2015.

The Women's World Cup tournament is held the year after the men's World Cup. France is the **host country** in 2019. Twenty-four teams will play for the cup.

The Women's World Cup **trophy** is made from marble, silver and gold.

World Cup facts

- Brazil has won the World Cup most times. It has five wins. Second equal are Italy and Germany, with four wins each.
- The USA and Germany have both won the Women's World Cup twice.
- At the 1958 World Cup in Sweden, French striker Just Fontaine scored an amazing 13 goals in six matches.
- The most goals scored in a World Cup match is 12. In the match, played in 1954, Austria beat Switzerland 7–5.
- The Jules Rimet **Trophy** was stolen before the tournament in England in 1966. It was found by a small black and white dog called Pickles!
- More than a billion people around the world watched the 2014 World Cup Final on television.

Glossary

dribble run along keeping a football close to the feet and passing players from the other team

extra time time played at the end of a game if both teams have the same number of goals

fan person who supports a football team

FIFA Fédération Internationale de Football Association (FIFA), which organizes the World Cup

free kick when a player is allowed to put the ball down and kick it without being tackled by a player from the other team

hat-trick three goals scored by the same player during a game of football

host country country where a World Cup tournament is played

trophy prize, normally a cup or shield, given to a person or team that wins a tournament

zone another word for an area

Find out more

Books

Stars of the World Cup, Illugi Jokulsson (Artabras, 2014)
Wicked World Cup, Michael Coleman (Scholastic, 2010)
World Cup Heroes (World Cup Fever series), Michael Hurley (Raintree, 2014)

Websites

www.fifa.com/worldcup/index.html
The official World Cup section of the FIFA website
www.fifa.com/fifa-tournaments/archive/worldcup/index.html
All the facts you need about World Cup games of the past

Index

2018 World Cup 14
competitions 6
England team 9, 10, 13
extra time 12
fair play 22
fans 12, 16, 17, 22, 26, 27
Fédération Internationale de Football Association (FIFA) 4, 9, 14, 26
Golden Ball award 23
Golden Boot award 23
Golden Glove award 23
hat-tricks 10
history 8
host countries 7, 14, 16, 18, 19, 29
Hurst, Geoff 10
Maradona, Diego 13
Moore, Bobby 9
opening ceremonies 18, 27
Pelé 11
penalty shootouts 20, 21
Russia 26
stadiums 15, 17, 27
sudden death 20
trophies 5, 9, 22, 25, 29, 30
Women's World Cup 5, 28, 29, 30
World Cup 2018 7, 14, 26
World Cup Final 10, 13, 24, 25, 27, 30